Ornaments of Fire

THE WORLD'S BEST 101 SHORT
POEMS AND FRAGMENTS

Selected and Edited by

EDD
WHEELER

FOREWORD BY ROBERT FRIEND

DRAWINGS BY DURFÉE McJOYNT

FITHIAN PRESS, SANTA BARBARA, 1994

To, in alphabetical order,
Catherine, Diana and Emily.

Copyright © 1994 Edd Wheeler
All rights reserved
Printed in the United Satates of America

Book design by Eric Larson

Published by
FITHIAN PRESS
A Division of Daniel and Daniel, Publishers, Inc.
Post Office Box 1525
Santa Barbara, CA 93120

LIBRARY OF CONGRESS CATALOGING-IN-PUBLICATION DATA
Ornaments of fire : the world's best 101 short poems and fragments /
    edited by Edd Wheeler.
        p. cm.
    Includes index.
    ISBN 1-56474-071-4
    1. Poetry—Collections. I. Wheeler, Edd.
PQ6101.076   1994
808.81—dc20   93-26419
                                                   CIP

CONTENTS

Call them felicity or presumptuousness
Call me Ishmael

FOREWORD

I have always liked the idea of the 100 best this and the 100 best that. And here, in actuality, is a selection of "The World's Best 101 Short Poems and Fragments." I shall not quibble about that extra *one,* nor shall I submit to another quibble: that this list represents the taste and judgment of one man alone. It does; that is part of its charm, part of its value. Arbitrary? Of course! The chief question to be asked is whether Judge Wheeler has evinced a convincing taste and judgment in his selection of the best. I believe he has, and the result is an anthology that will, I know, give great pleasure to, hopefully, a great number of people.

It is useless to object to what he has omitted. Given the enormous number of poems to choose from, it is possible to put together quite a few anthologies excellent as this one, anthologies that would include poems by, for example, Blake and Keats, which, for reasons of his own, Judge Wheeler has excluded. I, for one, would have liked to see Blake's "Ah Sun-flower" counterpointing the "Sunflower" by Anzai Hitoshi, a Japanese poet.

But it is precisely the editor's intention to include in his list poets other than "names." Not many of us in the West have heard of Hitoshi, or of a number of other foreign poets, whose translated poems appear here. Judge Wheeler has kept the promise explicit in his title, his wide-ranging taste finding for us poems that we may have missed otherwise, poems from the Oriental languages and from the European as well. Regarding English-writing poets, he has had the courage to include some scarcely heard of; and to my delight has been most partial to Mr. Anon, some of whose poems I had not known before.

—Robert Friend

INTRODUCTION

Poetry is (take your choice):
1. A juxtaposing of words
2. Best words arranged in best order
3. A spontaneous outpouring of emotion
4. Purest realization
5. A marriage of images and language too subtle for the intellect
6. Transmission of feelings experienced by the artist
7. A thing inward and subjective
8. Beautiful expression of some high truth
9. Knowledge conveyed with felicity
10. Exquisite metaphors on parade
11. Special use of language to send an extraordinary message
12. Words emotively used according to rules of some sort.

So much for an even dozen definitions, some being the distillations or partial expressions of the likes of Coleridge, Wordsworth, Keats, Yeats, Tolstoy and Pound (2 through 7 above, respectively), and others, the last four, homespun. Do they bring us nearer the tender vein of poetry? Probably not. The most common thread in these descriptions seems to be that poetry is a very special use of language—and a reliance upon it. When successful the language evokes special emotions. The skin may bristle, says Housman.

Poetry revisits old Truths or shows the world afresh. It is akin to pornography—and love. Like pornography it is not easily defined but is readily identifiable. And, as in love, you may never cease to be astonished by what is chosen by others.

I have chosen short poems. Beauty is fleeting. Immediacy is all. Even Homer may nod. Consistent with my approach, I will not offer amplified reasons. For spontaneous pleasure, we seem to turn more to the brilliant snapshot than to the wide tapestry. More means worse, Kingsley Amis observes.

Someone has ventured that literary achievement is attainable with a legacy of as few as ten good lines. An arbitrary figure. Along similar stripe, I arbitrarily have doubled that figure, with a little beside, in setting the upper limit for length of poems included here. Selections range from two to two dozen lines, the single exception being a 25-line excerpt from that most exceptional of biblical poets, the prophet Isaiah. Limits or rules only assume meaning to the extent they are selectively violated. Have I excluded sublime choices because of these artificial boundaries? Obviously so. Yet I do not seek the reader's forgiveness, only his brief enjoyment.

Also, without apology, I have included a few "poetic" fragments from prose (and history), as well as passages selected from longer poems. I have not transgressed frequently in this regard. What I lose in points with purists for this practice, I hope to recover in appeal to laymen, distinguished not only for their numbers but for a general tolerance of the quirkiness and risk-taking which may be found in these pages. Poems are introduced with commentary or identifiers, which I have strained to keep brief. Again, the purist may object, but some readers prefer a bit of slack with their salsa.

Twenty-six of the anthologized poems are anonymous. I personally find this fitting because many among us seldom know poems or poets or whole parts of the world by name, but only by the joy they provide or the pain visited and often in a narrow space. The final four of the book's poems are set explicitly in bed, the worst possible place for spilt milk. The book's poems also end as they begin, with a longing for company in bed. But in all of this, rest assured, no profundity is intended.

—E.W.

SMALL RAIN DOWN CAN RAIN

ANONYMOUS, *early sixteenth century*

Was ever wish, perhaps by mariner, more lonely or lyrical?

WESTERN WIND

Western wind, when will thou blow,
The small rain down can rain?
Christ, if my love were in my arms,
And I in my bed again.

Archibald MacLeish, *1933*

The earth and its tides of change wear upon us, until that time when we will wear the earth.

Seafarer

And learn O voyager to walk
The roll of earth, the pitch and fall
That swings across these trees those stars:
That swings the sunlight up the wall.

And learn upon these narrow beds
To sleep in spite of sea, in spite
Of sound the rushing planet makes:
And learn to sleep against this ground.

'UMARA OF MERV, *late tenth century*

An exquisite Persian lyric on stormy weather.

LASHED BY GUSTS THE LEAFY WILLOWS

Lashed by gusts the leafy willows
Are as drunkards reeling headlong.
Watch the crimson tulips waving
Bloodied sword-points in the dawn.

William Carlos Williams, *1923*

What depends? It is not overstatement to say, art and our informed perspective of the world.

THE RED WHEELBARROW

so much depends
upon

a red wheel
barrow

glazed with rain
water

beside the white
chickens.

E<small>ZRA</small> P<small>OUND</small>, *1916*

Beauty and surprise in a place of schedules and confusion.

IN A STATION OF THE METRO

The apparition of these faces in the crowd;
Petals on a wet, black bough.

T. E. HULME, *early twentieth century*

The little poem captures its country images as sharply as any camera.

AUTUMN

A touch of cold in the Autumn night—
I walked abroad,
And saw the ruddy moon lean over a hedge
Like a red-faced farmer.
I did not stop to speak, but nodded,
And round about were the wistful stars
With white faces like town children.

Yün Shou-p'ing, *late seventeenth century*

Purest condensation on condensation.

GREEN BANANA LEAVES

I sit here long, the lamp burns dim;
sound of rain, swept by the wind past my house.
The tears of the banana leaves, outside the window:
for whom are they falling tonight?

A. E. HOUSMAN, *1896*

From that spring of continual excitement which yielded A Shropshire Lad *comes this seemingly effortless jewel.*

WITH RUE MY HEART IS LADEN

With rue my heart is laden
    For golden friends I had,
For many a rose-lipt maiden
    And many a lightfoot lad.

By brooks too broad for leaping
    The lightfoot boys are laid;
The rose-lipt girls are sleeping
    In fields where roses fade.

Who has not seen the awakening in children—poignant almost beyond words, except these—that death is not sleep?

Jᴀɴᴇᴛ Wᴀᴋɪɴɢ

Beautifully Janet slept
Till it was deeply morning. She woke then
And thought about her dainty-feathered hen,
To see how it had kept.

. . .

"Old Chucky, old Chucky!" she cried,
Running across the world upon the grass
To Chucky's house, and listening. But alas,
Her Chucky had died.

It was a transmogrifying bee
Came droning down on Chucky's old bald head
And sat and put the poison. It scarcely bled,
But how exceedingly

And purply did the knot
Swell with the venom and communicate
Its rigor! Now the poor comb stood up straight
But Chucky did not.

So there was Janet
Kneeling on the wet grass, crying her brown hen
(Translated far beyond the daughters of men)
To rise and walk upon it.

And weeping fast as she had breath
Janet implored us, "Wake her from her sleep!"
And would not be instructed in how deep
Was the forgetful kingdom of death.

MARTIAL, *first century*

This epigram expresses the poet's wit in a more gentle sense than was his custom.

THE BEE IN AMBER

The bee in amber,
entombed in a bead of nectar,
lies immured in the splendor
of his life's labors as a collector.

WILLIAM WORDSWORTH, *early nineteenth century*

None other than a preceding poet, Ransom, criticized the following as too obviously agreeable, which shows only that poets do not necessarily make good critics. Simple, bounding optimism asks for neither commentator nor approval.

WRITTEN IN MARCH

The cock is crowing,
The stream is flowing,
The small birds twitter,
The lake doth glitter,
The green field sleeps in the sun;
The oldest and youngest
Are at work with the strongest;
The cattle are grazing,
Their heads never raising:
There are forty feeding like one!

Like an army defeated
The snow hath retreated
And now doth fare ill
On the top of the bare hill;
The plowboy is whooping—anon—anon:
There's joy in the mountains;
There's life in the fountains;
Small clouds are sailing,
Blue sky prevailing;
The rain is over and gone!

HOW TIME EXPANDS

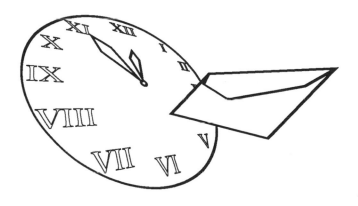

Ronald Wallace, *1992*

This more recent poem illustrates that one of the accomplishments of poetry is to lock, tentatively yet powerfully, the present (and future) with the past.

February 14

How time expands
to map the lost occasion:
A kiss, say, on the doorstep
of your sixteenth year,
that valentine to the future
that will always be arriving
at whatever address you've paid for
with such bright currency.

Or, likewise, contracts:
A decade, maybe, shrunk
to a scrap of paper,
an unintelligible scrawl
on the face of a torn envelope,
a message never sent.

ROBERT FRIEND, *mid-twentieth century*

The dreams of the deformed are easily as fertile for poetry as the aspirations of the erect, and equally filled with pathos.

THE HUNCHBACK

Within the house of mirrors
amazedly he sits
and studies in the mirrors
how well his hunchback fits.

He picks up his book of riddles
and tumbles his game of blocks.
How many tears in an onion?
How many springs in clocks?

Flies turn to bones of amber
when the spider spins itself,
and he sighs into the cobwebs
and the clock sighs on the shelf.

He treads his growing shadow,
and walks the endless round
along the edge of the mirror sea
where a hunchless ghost lies drowned.

A. E. HOUSMAN, *1896*

No ornament of fire hangs more brilliantly than this sunrise.

REVEILLE

Wake: the silver dusk returning
    Up the beach of darkness brims,
And the ship of sunrise burning
    Strands upon the eastern rims.

Wake: the vaulted shadow shatters,
    Trampled to the floor it spanned,
And the tent of night in tatters
    Straws the sky-pavilioned land.

Up, lad, up, 'tis late for lying:
    Hear the drums of morning play;
Hark, the empty highways crying
    'Who'll beyond the hills away?'

Towns and countries woo together,
    Forelands beacon, belfries call;
Never lad that trod on leather
    Lived to feast his heart with all.

Up, lad: thews that lie and cumber
    Sunlit pallets never thrive;
Morns abed and daylight slumber
    Were not meant for man alive.

Clay lies still, but blood's a rover;
    Breath's a ware that will not keep.
Up, lad: when the journey's over
    There'll be time enough to sleep.

JOHN PRESS, *mid-twentieth century*

Is the child's cry here that of infant fever or a vision of last things?

FAREWELL

Mary, daughter of King James I, when dying at the age of three, cried aloud: "I go, I go, away I go."

The smell of death was in the air
And, as the candles guttered low,
Her pain became a mounting tide
Which dragged her in its undertow.
She watched the world recede and cried:
"I go, I go, away I go."

This was a cry of pure despair
From one too innocent to know
That web of words we spin to cloak
The nakedness which Truth would show.
It was her dying wisdom spoke:
"I go, I go, away I go."

Even the glibbest courtier there
Was dumb to say it was not so.
How strange that, in a moment's space,
A child should into knowledge grow
And cry, by God's, or terror's, grace:
"I go, I go, away I go."

ANONYMOUS, *c. second century* B.C.

From the Greek epitaph of a young woman in Ptolemaic Egypt.

FOR TWICE TEN YEARS

For twice ten years my father provided for me,
nor did I even complete the rite
of the bridal chamber and bed,
nor did my body lie in the couch,
nor was there an allnight knocking
by girls of my age on the cedar doors.

ANONYMOUS, *sixteenth century*

An Elizabethan epitaph. Modernized spelling.

HERE LIES, THE LORD HAVE MERCY UPON HER

Here lies, the Lord have mercy upon her,
One of her majesty's maids of honour:
She was young, slender, and pretty,
She died a maid, the more the pity.

MORRIS WEISENTHAL, *mid-twentieth century*

Poems (this included) have commonly appeared on the editorial page of The New York Times *in this century; but poetry of such delicacy and sadness as here is hardly commonplace, in* The Times *or elsewhere.*

SMALL ELEGY

Say that she was young, awkward and bold—
Light matured her virtues some few summers
Then set her down; oh the promise
Of her dawn, the wide expectant eye.

Or write of her voice, uncertain as a reed
But supple with high faith; death stopped
It. Now the riderless seasons
Race and change, shrouded in speed.

ANONYMOUS, *fifteenth century*

A now-destroyed painting in a monastery at Avignon depicted a dead woman, enveloped in a shroud and with worms gnawing her bowels. The following, translated by Johan Huizinga, was inscribed at the foot of the painting.

[ONCE I WAS BEAUTIFUL ABOVE ALL WOMEN]

Once I was beautiful above all women
But by death I became like this,
My flesh was very beautiful, fresh and soft,
Now it is altogether turned to ashes.
My body was very pleasing and very pretty,
I used frequently to dress in silk,
Now I must rightly be quite nude.
I was dressed in grey fur and miniver,
I lived in a great palace as I wished,
Now I am lodged in this little coffin.
My room was adorned with fine tapestry,
Now my grave is enveloped in cobwebs.

JOHN CROWE RANSOM, *1927*

Mutability stalks the world but something equally inexorable is afoot. The young practice youth because it is their nature.

BLUE GIRLS

Twirling your blue skirts, traveling the sward
Under the towers of your seminary,
Go listen to your teachers old and contrary
Without believing a word.

Tie the white fillets then about your lustrous hair
And think no more of what will come to pass
Than bluebirds that go walking on the grass
And chattering on the air.

Practice your beauty, blue girls, before it fail;
And I will cry with my loud lips and publish
Beauty which all our power shall never establish,
It is so frail.

For I could tell you a story which is true:
I know a lady with a terrible tongue,
Blear eyes fallen from blue,
All her perfections tarnished—yet it is not long
Since she was lovelier than any of you.

FRANCOIS VILLON, *c. 1460*

From The Testament *comes this shuddering image. The words are those of an old Helmet-seller wishing for her former beauty.*

THE TESTAMENT

. . .

"The delicate little shoulders
The long arms and slender hands
The small breasts, the full buttocks
High, broad, perfectly built
For holding the jousts of love
The wide loins and the sweet quim
Set over thick firm thighs
In its own little garden?

"The forehead lined, the hair gray
The eyebrows all fallen out, the eyes clouded
Which threw those bright glances
That felled many a poor devil
The nose hooked far from beauty
The ears hairy and lopping down
The cheeks washed out, dead and pasty
The chin furrowed, the lips just skin.

"This is what human beauty comes to
The arms short, the hands shriveled
The shoulders all hunched up

The breasts? Shrunk in again
The buttocks gone the way of the tits
The quim? aagh! As for the thighs
They aren't thighs now but sticks
Speckled all over like sausages."

.   .   .

KONSTANTIN SIMONOV, 1941

The missing haunt us still, always have, always will.

JUST WAIT FOR ME

Just wait for me and I'll return.
But wait, oh, wait with all your might...
Wait when your heart is saddened by
The pouring rains, the sallow light.
Wait when the wind heaps up the snow,
Wait when the air is dry and hot.
Wait when the rest no longer wait
For those whom they too soon forgot.
Wait when the letters fail to come,
Wait on, through dread and through despair,
When those who wait together end
Their waiting and turn elsewhere.

.   .   .

Just wait for me and I'll return,
To spite all deaths that men can die.
Let those who gave up waiting say:
"It was his luck"—that is a lie.
It is not theirs to understand
Who gave up waiting, wearily,
How under fire I was safe,
Since, waiting, you protected me.

And none but you and I will know
How I escaped the thrust of fate—
Simply because, better than all
The others, you knew how to wait.

EMILY DICKINSON, *c. 1863*

Never have so many interjections (twenty-three) formed such a cohesive and articulate utterance. The conclusion even anticipates an interjection to follow—God's? Even at a time of national calamity, this poetess' head was always toward eternity.

BECAUSE I COULD NOT STOP FOR DEATH

Because I could not stop for Death—
He kindly stopped for me—
The Carriage held but just Ourselves—
And Immortality.

We slowly drove—He knew no haste
And I had put away
My labor and my leisure too,
For His Civility—

We passed the School, where Children strove
At Recess—in the Ring—
We passed the Fields of Gazing Grain—
We passed the Setting Sun—

Or rather—He passed Us—
The Dews drew quivering and chill—
For only Gossamer, my Gown—
My Tippet—only Tulle—

We paused before a House that seemed
A Swelling of the Ground—
The Roof was scarcely visible—
The Cornice—in the Ground—

Since then—'tis Centuries—and yet
Feels shorter than the Day
I first surmised the Horses' Heads
Were toward Eternity—

ANONYMOUS, *after 1740*

There were listeners —and doubts—before the days of radio telescopes.

HELEN'S EYE

Troy's towering roof has tumbled;
Helen's eyes are filled with dust.
Above the impermanent slaughter
I murmur at past tapestries,
The persistence of lips and saffron robes.
But between the wafer moon
And black holes in the sky,
The past murmurs back something
Foreign as a bird in Helen's eye.

WALT WHITMAN, *1865*

The stars may collapse into themselves but not into columns.

WHEN I HEARD THE LEARN'D ASTRONOMER

When I heard the learn'd astronomer,
When the proofs, the figures, were ranged in columns
      before me,
When I was shown the charts and diagrams, to add,
      divide, and measure them,
When I sitting heard the astronomer where he
      lectured with much applause in the lecture-
      room,
How soon unaccountable I became tired and sick,
Till rising and gliding out I wander'd off by myself,
In the mystical moist night-air, and from time to time,
Look'd up in perfect silence at the stars.

WILLIAM SHAKESPEARE, *c. 1611*

From The Tempest.

OUR REVELS NOW ARE ENDED

Our revels now are ended. These our actors,
As I foretold you, were all spirits and
Are melted into air, into thin air,
And, like the baseless fabric of this vision,
The cloud-capp'd towers, the gorgeous palaces,
The solemn temples, the great globe itself,
Yea, all which it inherit, shall dissolve
And, like this insubstantial pageant faded,
Leave not a rack behind. We are such stuff
As dreams are made on, and our little life
Is rounded with a sleep.

LOVE POEMS

ANONYMOUS, *early fourteenth century*

A celebration, not a boast.

ALL NIGHT BY THE ROSE

All night by the rose, rose—
All night by the rose I lay;
Dared I not the rose to steal,
And yet I bore the flower away.

ROBERT HERRICK, *seventeenth century*

Never has clinging garb been better described.

UPON JULIA'S CLOTHES

Whenas in silks my Julia goes,
Then, then (me thinks) how sweetly flows
That liquefaction of her clothes.

Next, when I cast mine eyes and see
That brave vibration each way free;
O how that glittering taketh me!

ANONYMOUS, *c. 1602*

A sliver of mild Elizabethan erotica.

MY LOVE IN HER ATTIRE

My love in her attire doth show her wit,
It doth so well become her:
For every season she hath dressings fit,
For winter, spring, and summer.
No beauty she doth miss,
When all her robes are on;
But Beauty's self she is,
When all her robes are gone.

ANONYMOUS, *c. third century* B.C.

The Song of Songs 4:9-14. The New English Bible.

YOU HAVE STOLEN MY HEART, MY SISTER

You have stolen my heart, my sister,
you have stolen it, my bride,
with one of your eyes, with one jewel of your
necklace.
How beautiful are your breasts, my sister, my bride!
Your love is more fragrant than wine,
and your perfumes sweeter than any spices.
Your lips drop sweetness like the honeycomb, my
bride,
syrup and milk are under your tongue,
and your dress has the scent of Lebanon.
Your two cheeks are an orchard of pomegranates,
an orchard full of rare fruits:
spikenard and saffron, sweet-cane and cinnamon
with every incense-bearing tree,
myrrh and aloes
with all the choicest spices.
My sister, my bride, is a garden close-locked,
a garden close-locked, a fountain sealed.

Anonymous, *c. third century* B.C.

The Song of Songs 5:10-16. The New English Bible.

My Beloved Is Fair and Ruddy

My beloved is fair and ruddy,
    a paragon among ten thousand.
His head is gold, finest gold;
    his locks are like palm-fronds.
His eyes are like doves beside brooks of water,
    splashed by the milky water
    as they sit where it is drawn.
His cheeks are like beds of spices or chests full of
        perfumes;
his lips are lilies, and drop liquid myrrh;
his hands are golden rods set in topaz;
his belly a plaque of ivory overlaid with lapis lazuli.
His legs are pillars of marble in sockets of finest gold;
his aspect is like Lebanon, noble as cedars.
His whispers are sweetness itself, wholly desirable.
Such is my beloved, such is my darling,
    daughters of Jerusalem.

BEN JONSON, *1616*

Rare Ben Jonson, indeed.

SONG: TO CELIA

Drink to me only with thine eyes,
And I will pledge with mine;
Or leave a kiss but in the cup,
And I'll not look for wine.
The thirst that from the soul doth rise,
Doth ask a drink divine:
But might I of Jove's nectar sup,
I would not change for thine.

I sent thee late a rosy wreath,
Not so much honoring thee,
As giving it a hope, that there
It could not withered be.
But thou thereon did'st only breathe,
And sent'st it back to me;
Since when it grows and smells, I swear,
Not of itself, but thee.

ANONYMOUS, *fourteenth century*

ANONYMOUS, *fourteenth century*

This lightly risqué love lyric was probably sung by a minstrel. "Ind" is indigo, dark blue.

I HAVE A NOBLE COCKEREL

I have a noble cockerel
Whose crowing starts my day:
He makes me get up early
My morning prayer to say.

I have a noble cockerel
Of lofty pedigree:
His comb is of red coral,
His tail jet-black to see.

I have a noble cockerel;
He comes of gentle kind:
His comb is of red coral,
His tail is of Ind.

His legs are all of azure,
Graceful, soft, and slim:
His spurs are silver white
Deep to the root of him.

His eyes are of crystal,
Sweetly set in amber;
And every night he perches
In my lady's chamber.

KISA'I OF MERV, *late tenth century*

As with love, the poem's glow is not subject to clear focus; but few can doubt that it will shine for yet another thousand years.

BEAUTY'S QUEEN BY LOVERS GUARDED

Beauty's queen by lovers guarded,
You whose cheeks the moon doth glass,
Where you glance, narcissus blooming;
The moon rising, where you pass!

Oh, your face and hair—the fairest
Book of white and black is this!
Cheek and tress are sin and penance,
Lip and eye are bale and bliss.

Theodore Roethke, *1954*

A literate and delicious poem of, yet still, natural processes; though one wonders if it could be published today, as originally, in a leading women's magazine.

I Knew a Woman

I knew a woman, lovely in her bones,
When small birds sighed, she would sigh back at them;
Ah, when she moved, she moved more ways than one:
The shapes a bright container can contain!
Of her choice virtues only gods should speak,
Or English poets who grew up on Greek
(I'd have them sing in chorus, cheek to cheek).

. . .

She was the sickle; I, poor I, the rake,
Coming behind her for her pretty sake
(But what prodigious mowing we did make).

Love likes a gander, and adores a goose:
Her full lips pursed, the errant note to seize;
She played it quick, she played it light and loose,
My eyes, they dazzled at her flowing knees;
Her several parts could keep a pure repose,
Or one hip quiver with a mobile nose
(She moved in circles, and those circles moved).

Let seed be grass, and grass turn into hay:
I'm martyr to a motion not my own;
What's freedom for? To know eternity.
I swear she cast a shadow white as stone.
But who would count eternity in days?
These old bones live to learn her wanton ways:
(I measure time by how a body sways).

MATTHEW ARNOLD, *1867*

Whatever else this justly famous poem may be, it is also poetry of love. The first and final stanzas are given.

DOVER BEACH

The sea is calm tonight.

The tide is full, the moon lies fair

Upon the straits; on the French coast the light

Gleams and is gone; the cliffs of England stand,

Glimmering and vast, out in the tranquil bay.

Come to the window, sweet is the night-air!

Only, from the long line of spray

Where the sea meets the moon-blanched land,

Listen! you hear the grating roar

Of pebbles which the waves draw back, and fling,

At their return, up the high strand,

Begin, and cease, and then again begin,

With tremulous cadence slow, and bring

The eternal note of sadness in.

.   .   .

Ah, love, let us be true
To one another! for the world, which seems
To lie before us like a land of dreams,
So various, so beautiful, so new,
Hath really neither joy, nor love, nor light,
Nor certitude, nor peace, nor help for pain;
And we are here as on a darkling plain
Swept with confused alarms of struggle and flight,
Where ignorant armies clash by night.

FUJIWARA NO YOSHITSUNE, *c. 1200*

This tanka, five lines with syllabic count 5-7-5-7-7, was written by a tutor to the Japanese imperial family.

ON YOUR SLEEPING MAT

On your sleeping mat
This night when the crickets' cry
    Is predicting frost
Must you spread only one side
Of your robe for you alone?

ANONYMOUS, *early sixth century B.C.*

Often attributed to Sappho.

THE MOON HAS SET

The moon has set,
and the Pleiades as well;
in the deep middle of the night
the time is passing,
and I lie alone.

ANONYMOUS, *prior to nineteenth century*

This is a modern version of the lyrics of an immemorial folk song from the west of England, though the earliest written version dates only from the late nineteenth century.

THE UNQUIET GRAVE

Cold blows the wind to my true love,
    And a few small drops of rain;
I never had but one true love;
    And in greenwood he was slain.

I'll do as much for my true love
    As any young girl may;
I'll sit and weep down by his grave
    For twelve months and a day.

But when twelve months were done and gone,
    This young man, he arose:
What makes you weep down by my grave?
    I can't take my repose.

One kiss of your lily-white lips,
    One kiss is all I crave;
One kiss of your lily-white lips
    And return back to your grave.

My lips, they are as cold as clay;
  My breath is earthy and strong;
If you would kiss my lily-white lips,
  Your days would not be long.

My time be long, my time be short,
  Tomorrow or today;
Sweet Christ in heaven, hold my song
  And take my life away.

GEORGE GORDON, LORD BYRON, *1817*

Love eclipsed by time, yet freed of it by the poem.

SO WE'LL GO NO MORE A-ROVING

1

So we'll go no more a -roving
   So late into the night,
Though the heart be still as loving,
   And the moon be still as bright.

2

For the sword outwears its sheath,
   And the soul wears out the breast,
And the heart must pause to breathe,
   And Love itself have rest.

3

Though the night was made for loving,
   And the day returns too soon,
Yet we'll go no more a-roving
   By the light of the moon.

JOHN CLARE, *nineteenth century.*

A fragment of the Truth, but is not the last word on love... a word?

FRAGMENT

Language has not the power to speak what love
      indites:
The soul lies buried in the ink that writes.

ROBERT NYE, *1969*

Familiarity here breeds not contempt but a relentless candor.

FAMILIAR TERMS

You say I love you for your lies?
　　But that's not true.
I love your absent-hearted eyes—
　　And so do you.

You say you love me for my truth?
　　But that's a lie.
You love my tongue because it's smooth—
　　And so do I.

You say they love who lie this way?
　　I don't agree.
They lie in love and waste away—
　　And so do we.

GOD AND COUNTRY

ANONYMOUS, *c. 540 B.C.*

The Book of the Prophet Isaiah 40:21-24, 28-31. The New English Bible.

DO YOU NOT KNOW, HAVE YOU NOT

HEARD

Do you not know, have you not heard,
were you not told long ago,
have you not perceived ever since the world began,
that God sits throned on the vaulted roof of earth,
    whose inhabitants are like grasshoppers?
  He stretches out the skies like a curtain,
  he spreads them out like a tent to live in;
  he reduces the great to nothing
  and makes all earth's princes less than nothing.
Scarcely are they planted, scarcely sown,
scarcely have they taken root in the earth,
    before he blows upon them and they wither away,
    and a whirlwind carries them off like chaff.

  · · ·

Do you not know, have you not heard?
The LORD, the everlasting God, creator of the wide
      world,
    grows neither weary nor faint;
    no man can fathom his understanding.

He gives vigour to the weary,
new strength to the exhausted.
Young men may grow weary and faint,
even in their prime they may stumble and fall;
but those who look to the LORD will win new
strength,
they will grow wings like eagles;
they will run and not be weary,
they will march on and never grow faint.

ANONYMOUS, *prior to sixteenth century*

The following, from the Sarum Missal and with modernized spelling, was part of the liturgy of the English church in late-medieval times and thus predates the Book of Common Prayer.

SARUM MISSAL

God be in my head,
And in my understanding;

God be in my eyes,
And in my looking;

God be in my mouth,
And in my speaking;

God be in my heart,
And in my thinking;

God be at my end,
And at my departing.

HENRY WADSWORTH LONGFELLOW,

mid-nineteenth century

Saint Teresa, sixteenth-century Spanish nun, wished to be called Teresa of Jesus, with whom, along with angels, she was said to speak in electric visions.

SANTA TERESA'S BOOK-MARK

Let nothing disturb thee,

Nothing affright thee;

All things are passing;

God never changeth;

Patient endurance

Attaineth to all things;

Who God possesseth

In nothing is wanting;

Alone God sufficeth.

Rainer Maria Rilke, *early twentieth century*

*There is no reason to believe that God is impressed by human attempts at
eloquence or playfulness, but if Rilke's expression of vulnerability does not
somehow register there can be no hope.*

"What Will You Do, God?"

What will you do, God, when I die?
I am your jar (if cracked, I lie?)
Your well-spring (if the well go dry?)
I am your craft, your vesture, I,
you lose your purport, losing me.

When I go, your cold house will be
empty of words that made it sweet.
I am the sandals your bare feet
will seek and long for, wearily.

Your cloak will fall from aching bones.
Your glance, that my warm cheeks have cheered
as with a cushion, long endeared,
will wonder at a loss so weird,
and when the sun has disappeared,
lie in the lap of alien stones.

What will you do, God? I'm afeared.

WILLIAM C. DIX, *late nineteenth century*

The third stanza of five in the hymn.

ALLELUIA! BREAD OF HEAVEN

Alleluia! Bread of Heaven,
    thou on earth our food, our stay!
Alleluia! here the sinful
    flee to thee from day to day:
Intercessor, friend of sinners,
    earth's Redeemer, plead for me,
where the songs of all the sinless
    sweep across the crystal sea.

MEIR BEN ISAAC NEHERAI, c. 1050

From A Book of Jewish Thoughts Selected for the Sailors and Soldiers of England *(First World War)*.

COULD WE WITH INK THE OCEAN FILL

Could we with ink the ocean fill,

Were every blade of grass a quill,

Were the world of parchment made,

And every man a scribe by trade,

To write the love

Of God above

Would drain the ocean dry;

Nor would the scroll

Contain the whole,

Though stretched from sky to sky.

ANONYMOUS, *c. 1704*

Prayer of a common soldier before the battle of Blenheim; quoted in John Newman's Apologia.

[PRAYER]

O God, if there be a God,

save my soul, if I have a soul.

Anonymous, *c. 1942*

From "A Soldier—His Prayer," in Poems from the Desert *(1944);*
poem written by a member of the British Eighth Army, during the Battle
of El Alamein, and found in a slit trench.

A Soldier—His Prayer

Stay with me God. The night is dark,

The night is cold: my little spark

Of courage dies. The night is long;

Be with me, God, and make me strong.

SIMONIDES, c. 480 B.C.

*Three translations of the epitaph on the Spartans at Thermopylae, called
by Ruskin the noblest group of words uttered by man.*

[EPITAPH]

Go tell the Spartans,
    thou who passest by,
That here, obedient to their laws,
    we lie.[1]

O passer by,
    tell the Lacedaemonians
    that we lie here
    obeying their orders.[2]

We lie here,
    having given our lives
    to save all Hellas,
    when she stood on a razor's edge.[3]

[1] *Translated by W.L. Bowles.*
[2] *Translated by J.W. Mackail*
[3] *Inscription on a gift to President Truman "from Grateful Greece"
commemorating the Truman Doctrine.*

GLADYS ELY, *mid-twentieth century*

Through containment and marvelous control of strong emotion, the poem builds to its conclusion, a fit epitaph for the soldier—or jobbist.

VARIATIONS ON SIMONIDES

Stranger, tell the Spartans we lie here,

Obedient to the rigorous Spartan star.

Traveler, tell them how the gates were passed,

Through traitors, not through us who fought and lost.

Stranger, say we kept the iron gain

Of the black broth of comrades and of men.

Do not say we thought we gave our breath

To save the repressive country of our youth.

Report, as we were bade, we made our end,

Not dreaming that all Hellas was our land.

We combed our hair and raised our swords to die.

We left our sons to flesh a further day.

Hot gates froze shut the sequences of time:

We bleed in a laconic epigram.

A narrow country narrowly defines.

We did our narrow best in narrow lines.

MAMERCUS, *fourth century B.C.*

The despot Mamercus in Sicily had this delicious insult of defeated adversaries inscribed upon their shields, which he dedicated to the gods.

[INSULT]

These purple-painted shields of gold
and ivory and electrum
we took with little shields
that cost us cheap.

LAURENCE BINYON, *c. 1920*

The fourth stanza of Binyon's poem is given as inscribed on the British Museum War Memorial.

FOR THE FALLEN

They shall grow not old
As we that are left grow old
Age shall not weary them
Nor the years condemn
At the going down of the sun
And in the morning
We will remember them

WILHELM KLEMM, *c. 1914*

Epic battles were fought at the Marne in 1914 and 1918.

THE BATTLE OF THE MARNE

Slowly the stones begin to rouse themselves and to talk.
The grasses stiffen to green metal. Woods,
Thick, crouching ambush, devour distant columns.
The sky, that chalk-white secret, threatens to burst.
Two colossal hours unroll into minutes.
The empty horizon swells.

My heart is as big as Germany and France together,
Pierced by all the shots of the world.
The battery heaves its leonine voice
Six times into the distance. Grenades are howling.
Silence. Far off, smokes the fire of the infantry,
For days, for weeks.

ANONYMOUS, *ninth century* B.C.

A stirring assembly of Chinese martial clans emits an energy that has lasted almost three millennia.

HOW GOES THE NIGHT?

How goes the night?
Midnight has still to come.
Down in the court the torch is blazing bright;
I hear far off the throbbing of the drum.

How goes the night?
The night is not yet gone.
I hear the trumpets blowing on the height;
The torch is paling in the coming dawn.

How goes the night?
The night is past and done.
The torch is smoking in the morning light,
The dragon banner floating in the sun.

OF ANIMALS AND MEN

ALCMAN, *seventh century* B.C.

The founder of Doric lyric poetry describes the stillness of a Spartan night.

NOW SLEEP THE MOUNTAIN PEAKS AND RAVINES

Now sleep the mountain peaks and ravines,

ridges and torrent streams, all creeping things

that black night nourishes,

wild upland beasts and the race of bees,

and monsters in the gulfs of the dark-gleaming

sea; now sleep the tribes of long-winged birds.

ANONYMOUS, *twelfth century*

From an ancient Norse poem, The Proverb Song (Havamal).

CATTLE DIE

Cattle die,
Friends die,
Thou thyself shalt die,
I know a thing
That never dies,
Judgment over the dead.

ALFRED, LORD TENNYSON, *1851*

Motion, force, and loneliness—in inverse order.

THE EAGLE

He clasps the crag with crooked hands;
Close to the sun in lonely lands,
Ring'd with the azure world, he stands.

The wrinkled sea beneath him crawls;
He watches from his mountain walls,
And like a thunderbolt he falls.

PIUVKAQ, *early twentieth century*

Eskimo song among Canadian Eskimo material collected by Knud Rasmussen.

DELIGHT IN SINGING

It's wonderful
to make up songs:
but all too many of them fail.

It's wonderful
to have your wishes granted:
but all too often
they slip by.

It's wonderful
to hunt reindeer:
but all too seldom
you succeed,
standing like a bright fire
on the plain.

JAMES RUSSELL LOWELL, *late ninetenth century*

An auspex in ancient times prophesied based upon the observation of birds in action.

AUSPEX

My heart, I cannot still it
Nest that had song-birds in it;
And when the last shall go,
The dreary days, to fill it,
Instead of lark or linnet,
Shall whirl dead leaves and snow.

Had they been swallows only,
Without the passion stronger
That skyward longs and sings—
Woe's me, I shall be lonely
When I can feel no longer
The impatience of their wings!

A moment, sweet delusion,
Like birds the brown leaves hover;
But it will not be long
Before their wild confusion
Fall wavering down to cover
The poet and his song.

SERGEY YESENIN, *early twentieth century*

Expansive "wooden Russia" as recounted, or imagined, in the last days of the czars.

FIELD UPON FIELD UPON FIELD

Field upon field upon field,
The provinces' dead hand.
Yesterday lights on my heart,
Within—bright Russia stands.

The miles come whistling
Off my horse's hooves like birds
And the sun is casting
Handfuls of rain on my head.

O land of savage flood
And gentle springtime pressures.
For schooling all I had
Was dawn and the stars.

And the winds for me were a bible
To read in and to muse,
While by my side Isaiah,
Tended his golden cows.

LEIGH HUNT, *early nineteenth century*

From the conclusion of the third of "Three Sonnets" come these unlikely words of fish to man, but the perspective and the message are shimmering.

THREE SONNETS

.   .   .

Man's life is warm, glad, sad, 'twixt loves and graves,
Boundless in hope, honoured with pangs austere,
Heaven-gazing; and his angel-wings he craves:
The fish is swift, small-needing, vague yet clear,
A cold, sweet, silver life, wrapped in round waves,
Quickened with touches of transporting fear.

ANONYMOUS, *third century B.C.*

This description of Gautama, the Buddha, by his mother, Queen Gautami, is from Buddhist scriptures and arranged here as poetry.

[GAUTAMI WEEPING]

Beautiful, soft, black, and all in great waves,

growing each from its own special root,

those hairs of his are tossed on the ground,

worthy to be encircled by a royal diadem.

With his long arms and lion-gait,

his bull-like eye, and his beauty bright like gold,

his broad chest, and his voice deep as a drum or a

       cloud,—

should such a hero as this dwell in a hermitage?

MATTHEW ARNOLD, *1857*

As clear and biting as any picture of life in miniature is this passage.

RUGBY CHAPEL

. . .

What is the course of the life
Of mortal men on the earth?—
Most men eddy about
Here and there—eat and drink,
Chatter and love and hate,
Gather and squander, are raised
Aloft, are hurled in the dust.
Striving blindly, achieving
Nothing; and, then they die—
Perish; and no one asks
Who or what they have been,
More than he asks what waves
In the moonlit solitudes mild
Of the midmost Ocean, have swelled,
Foamed for a moment, and gone.

. . .

HENRY KING, *mid-seventeenth century*

The poet's rendering of the trajectory of life in a dozen brisk lines.

SUCH IS LIFE

Like to the falling of the star,
Or as the flights of eagles are,
Or like the fresh spring's gaudy hue,
Or silver drops of morning dew,
Or like a wind that chafes the flood,
Or bubbles which on water stood;
Even such is Man, whose borrowed light
Is straight called in, and paid to night.

The wind blows out, the bubble dies,
The spring entombed in autumn lies,
The dew dries up, the star is shot,
The flight is past, and Man forgot.

JOHN MASEFIELD, *mid-twentieth century*

Perspective, one of the few benefits of age, here yields wry affirmation.

AN EPILOGUE

I have seen flowers come in stony places
And kind things done by men with ugly faces,
And the gold cup won by the worst horse at the races,
So I trust, too.

LOST CAUSES

EDWIN MUIR, *mid-twentieth century*

> *Whatever this unsettling dialogue may yield, it does not yield directions,
> at least none comforting to the journeyer.*

THE WAY

Friend, I have lost the way.
The way leads on.
Is there another way?
The way is one.
I must retrace the track.
It's lost and gone.
Back, I must travel back!
None goes there, none.
Then I'll make here my place,
(The road runs on),
Stand still and set my face,
(The road leaps on),
Stay, here, for ever stay.
None stays here, none.
I cannot find the way.
The way leads on.
Oh places I have passed!
That journey's done.
And what will come at last?
The road leads on.

HOMER, *c. eighth century* B.C.

The Iliad *did not appear in even rudimentary written form before 550 B.C. These final lines from Samuel Butler's great nineteenth-century translation in prose are rearranged here in poetic form.*

[THE FUNERAL OF HECTOR]

Then when the child of morning rosy-fingered dawn
    appeared on the eleventh day,
    the people again assembled,
    round the pyre of mighty Hector.
When they were got together,
    they quenched the fire with wine wherever it was
        burning,
    and then his brothers and comrades with many a
        bitter tear
    gathered his white bones,
    wrapped them in soft robes of purple,
    and laid them in a golden urn,
    which they placed in a grave and covered
    over with large stones set close together.
Then they built a barrow hurriedly over it
    keeping guard on every side
    lest the Achaeans should attack them before they
        had finished
When they had heaped up the barrow
    they went back again into the city,
    and being well assembled they held high feast
    in the house of Priam their king.
Thus, then, did they celebrate
    the funeral of Hector tamer of horses.

J. K. Clark, *mid-twentieth century*

A poem of special meaning, not only for combat veterans but for anyone who, out of courage or necessity or both, has rolled the dice at hand for high stakes—and lost.

RETREAT

Now as we fall back from below the ridge,

Abandoning our hotly held positions,

We can lay aside the anguish of our fear

And assume the duller burden of ourselves.

For though our dead are carefully interred,

Their honor well established, and although

The military manuals positively state

That such assaults as ours can never win,

And though we knew the odds against success

Were infinite, still we must explain—

Explain the failure of the bayonet,

The fury of the enfilading fire,

Explain the lack of mortars and air cover.

We must explain, and once again explain,

That no defect of ours, no lack of courage,

No failure of the nerve or of the will

Repulsed our thrusts. We must refight this field

Forever on the ridges of our minds

And lose it always as we lost it here.

G. K. CHESTERTON, *early twentieth century*

So we all feel at times about those who govern or pretend to.

ELEGY IN A COUNTRY CHURCHYARD

The men that worked for England
They have their graves at home:
And bees and birds of England
About the cross can roam.

But they that fought for England,
Following a falling star,
Alas, alas for England
They have their graves afar.

And they that rule in England,
In stately conclave met,
Alas, alas for England
They have no graves as yet.

HERMANN GRAEBE, c. 1945

Can a Nazi engineer's eyewitness account of a wrenching atrocity be construed as poetry? Nowhere is it written that poetry may only evoke pleasure. The affidavit from which the following is taken was used at the Nuremberg trials.

[AFFIDAVIT]

"During the 15 minutes
that I stood near the pit
I heard no complaint or plea for mercy.
I watched a family...
An old woman with snow-white hair was holding
the one-year-old child in her arms and singing...
The child was cooing with delight.
The couple were looking on with tears
in their eyes. The father was holding
the hand of a boy... The father
pointed toward the sky, stroked his head,
and seemed to explain something to him.
At that moment the SS-man at the pit
shouted something to his comrade.
The latter counted off about 20 persons
and instructed them
to go behind the earth mound.
Among them was the family...
I remember a girl,
slim and with black hair,
who, as she passed close to me,
pointed to herself and said,
'23.' "

ANONYMOUS, *c. second century* B.C.

From a Greek inscription of Epicurean persuasion.

[EPICUREAN CONCLUSION]

I have what I ate,
I have lost what I left.
Philistion was right;
that is all life amounts to.

ANONYMOUS

A riddle and two seeming variants, ancient to sixteenth century.

[RIDDLE]

What we caught we threw away,
What we could not catch we kept.[1]

What wee gave, wee have;
What wee spent, wee had;
What wee kept, wee lost.[2]

That we spent, we had:
That we gave, we have:
That we left, we lost.[3]

[1] *Said to have vexed Homer to death.*
[2] *Epitaph on the Earl of Devonshire, died 1419.*
[3] *Variant of epitaph, as quoted by Edmund Spenser, late sixteenth century.*

CHIDIOCK TICHBORNE, *c. 1586*

Written by him in the Tower of London before his execution.

TICHBORNE'S ELEGY

My prime of youth is but a frost of cares,
My feast of joy is but a dish of pain,
My crop of corn is but a field of tares,
And all my good is but vain hope of gain;
The day is past, and yet I saw no sun,
And now I live, and now my life is done.

My tale was heard and yet it was not told,
My fruit is fallen and yet my leaves are green,
My youth is spent and yet I am not old,
I saw the world and yet I was not seen;
My thread is cut and yet it is not spun,
And now I live, and now my life is done.

I sought my death and found it in my womb,
I looked for life and saw it was a shade,
I trod the earth and knew it was my tomb,
And now I die, and now I was but made;
My glass is full, and now my glass is run,
And now I live, and now my life is done.

ANONYMOUS, *thirteenth century*

Translation of medieval students' Latin drinking song, revised in the eighteenth century.

LET US THEN REJOICE

Let us then rejoice,

While we are young.

After the pleasures of youth

And the tiresomeness of old age

Earth will hold us.

ANONYMOUS, *twelfth century B.C.*

A translation, from the Chinese, of possibly the most ancient of recorded drinking songs.

THE DEW IS HEAVY ON THE GRASS

The dew is heavy on the grass,
   At last the sun is set.
Fill up, fill up the cups of jade,
   The night's before us yet!

All night the dew will heavy lie
   Upon the grass and clover.
Too soon, too soon, the dew will dry,
   Too soon the night be over!

John W. Draper, *1876*

The words of an historian may sometimes be rendered as poetry of the highest order, as in this description of the sack of Constantinople in 1453.

[Last of the Roman Emperors]

Constantine Palaeologus, the last of the Roman
      emperors,
putting off his purple, that no man might
recognize and insult his corpse
when the catastrophe was over,
fell, as became a Roman emperor,
in the breach. After his death
resistance ceased, and the victorious Turks poured
into the town. To the Church of St. Sophia
there rushed a promiscuous crowd of women and
      children,
priests, monks, religious virgins, and—men.
Superstitious to the last,
in this supreme moment they expected
the fulfillment of a prophecy that,
when the Turks should have forced their way
to the square before that church,
their progress would be arrested,
for an angel with a sword in his hand
would descend from heaven and save
the city of the Lord. The Turks
burst into the square,
but the angel never came.

GIFTS OF PRICE AND THE MERELY BEAUTIFUL

KISA'I OF MERV, *late tenth century*

The most charming of countless tributes by Persian poets to their favorite
flower, the rose.

ROSES ARE A GIFT OF PRICE

Roses are a gift of price
Sent to us from Paradise;
More divine our nature grows
In the Eden of the rose.

Roses why for silver sell?
O rose merchant, fairly tell
What you buy instead of those
That is costlier than the rose.

William Shakespeare, *c. 1595*

From A Midsummer-Night's Dream.

I Know a Bank Where the Wild Thyme Blows

I know a bank where the wild thyme blows,
Where oxlips and the nodding violet grows,
Quite over-canopied with luscious woodbine,
With sweet musk-roses and with eglantine:
There sleeps Titania sometime of the night,
Lull'd in these flowers with dances and delight;
And there the snake throws her enamell'd skin,
Weed wide enough to wrap a fairy in:
And with the juice of this I'll streak her eyes,
And make her full of hateful fantasies.

ROBERT HERRICK, *seventeenth century*

Sorrow and joy, restraint and vitality, in the simplest of stanzas.

UPON PRUE HIS MAID

In this little urn is laid
Prewdence Baldwin (once my maid)
From whose happy spark here let
Spring the purple violet.

Anzai Hitoshi, *1955*

From Flower Shop *blossoms this commingling of East and West.*

SUNFLOWER

On the edge of a country road
I happened to meet
Van Gogh
Stupefied, standing hatless
In the sun's hot light.

Ah! A stream of blue sky
Over a deserted Dutch village!
But it's not just that. Everything
Becomes clearer
Only when I stand beside
This one flower.

ROBERT NYE, *1969*

A more elegant rendering of the truth in Joyce Kilmer's couplet: "Poems are made by fools like me, But only God can make a tree."

A PROPER PLACE

Outside my window
two tall witch-elms
toss their inspired
green heads in the sun
and lean together
whispering.

Trees make the world
a proper place.

A. E. HOUSMAN, *1896*

Any disbelief that such poignancy might be voiced by a 20-year-old is swept to the side by the stunning beauty of the poem.

LOVELIEST OF TREES

Loveliest of trees, the cherry now
Is hung with bloom along the bough,
And stands about the woodland ride
Wearing white for Eastertide.

Now, of my threescore years and ten,
Twenty will not come again,
And take from seventy springs a score,
It only leaves me fifty more.

And since to look at things in bloom
Fifty springs are little room,
About the woodlands I will go
To see the cherry hung with snow.

The firmament in a single and singular image.

MOONLIT NIGHT

A Landscape

There'll be a moon.
Already there's
a bit of it,
and now, in the air, a full moon is hanging.
Must be God
poking around
in the star chowder
with a marvelous silver spoon.

VLADIMIR SOLOUKHIN, *mid-twentieth century*

The fruit falls, and is consumed, in no deference to science.

THE APPLE

I am convinced that finally
Isaac Newton ate
The apple that taught him
The law of gravity.

The apple, born of Earth and Sun,
Came into being,
Sprang from the seed,
Ripened
(And before this bees flew to it,
Rain fell and a warm wind blew),
Not so much that it might drop
And by its direct motion demonstrate
That gravity exists,
But to become
            heavy and sweet,
To be admired and picked,
Its scent enjoyed—
And with its sweetness
To delight a Man.

WILLIAM WORDSWORTH, *1802*

The pulse and panorama of a great city are frozen in the poet's eye and under a majestically thin glaze of only a dozen or so somewhat traditional adjectives.

COMPOSED UPON WESTMINSTER BRIDGE

Earth has not anything to show more fair:
Dull would he be of soul who could pass by
A sight so touching in its majesty;
This City now doth, like a garment, wear
The beauty of the morning; silent, bare,
Ships, towers, domes, theaters, and temples lie
Open unto the fields, and to the sky;
All bright and glittering in the smokeless air.
Never did sun more beautifully steep
In his first splendor, valley, rock, or hill;
Ne'er saw I, never felt, a calm so deep!
The river glideth at his own sweet will:
Dear God! the very houses seem asleep;
And all that mighty heart is lying still!

EMILY DICKINSON, *c. 1866*

The poem instantly telescopes in on one of life's most stressful moments and then implodes.

THE BUSTLE IN A HOUSE

The Bustle in a House
The Morning after Death
Is solemnest of industries
Enacted upon Earth—

The Sweeping up the Heart
And putting Love away
We shall not want to use again
Until Eternity.

W. B. YEATS, *c. 1926*

The question posed at the end of this last stanza of the poem is as intoxicating, and vexing, as any in literature.

AMONG SCHOOL CHILDREN

.   .   .

Labour is blossoming or dancing where
The body is not bruised to pleasure soul,
Nor beauty born out of its own despair,
Nor blear-eyed wisdom out of midnight oil.
O chestnut-tree, great-rooted blossomer,
Are you the leaf, the blossom or the bole?
O body swayed to music, O brightening glance,
How can we know the dancer from the dance?

SPILT MILK

W.B. YEATS, *1933*

Spillage as certain as the years.

SPILT MILK

We that have done and thought,
That have thought and done,
Must ramble, and thin out
Like milk spilt on a stone.

MATTHEW PRIOR, *early eighteenth century*

This stanza is from Solomon. *Prior said that he was "only a poet by accident"—fortunate accident, fortunate us.*

LOOS'D BY DEVOURING TIME THE SILVER CORD

. . .

Loos'd by devouring Time the silver Cord
Dissever'd lies: unhonor'd from the Board
The Crystal Urn, when broken, is thrown by;
And apter Utensils their Place supply.
These Things and Thou must share One equal Lot;
Dye and be lost, corrupt and be forgot;
While still another, and another Race
Shall now supply, and now give up the Place.
From Earth all came, to Earth must all return;
Frail as the Cord, and brittle as the Urn.

. . .

V<small>IRGIL</small>, *c. 20 B.C.*

This is not moroseness but urgency, the urgency of unresting industry;
loosely translated by Justice Oliver Wendell Holmes.

D<small>EATH</small> P<small>LUCKS</small> M<small>Y</small> E<small>AR</small>

Death plucks my ear and says,

"Live—I am coming."

ANONYMOUS, *prior to twentieth century*

From an old Eskimo song, and epilogue to the movie, Never Cry Wolf *(1982).*

I THINK OVER AGAIN MY SMALL ADVENTURES

I think over again my small adventures,
My fears,
Those small ones that seemed so big,
For all the vital things
I had to get and to reach;
And yet there is only one great thing,
The only thing,
To live to see the great day that dawns
And the light that fills the world.

ANONYMOUS, *c. 1746*

Epitaph on blacksmith William Strange, in Nettlebed churchyard, England.

MY SLEDGE AND ANVIL LIE DECLINED

My sledge and anvil like declined

My bellows too have lost their wind

My fire's extinct, my forge decayed,

And in the Dust my Vice is laid

My coals are spent, my iron's gone

My Nails are Drove, My Work is done.

ANONYMOUS, *nineteenth century*

Poetry need not always be bound in high seriousness; from a former epitaph, now destroyed, in Bushey churchyard, England.

HERE LIES A POOR WOMAN

Here lies a poor woman who always was tired,
For she lived in a place where help wasn't hired.
Her last words on earth were, Dear friends I am going
Where washing ain't done nor sweeping nor sewing,
And everything there is exact to my wishes,
For there they don't eat and there's no washing of
       dishes...
Don't mourn for me now, don't mourn for me never,
For I'm going to do nothing for ever and ever.

CHAO MENG-FU, *early fourteenth century*

Chinese poets of antiquity generally were master painters and calligraphers.

AN ADMONITION TO MYSELF

Your teeth are loose, your head is bald,
            you're sixty-three years old;
every aspect of your life
            should make you feel ashamed.
All that's left that interests you
            are the products of your brush:
leave them behind to give the world
            something to talk about.

ANATOLY STEIGER, *after 1930*

Bare branch and bare truth.

UNTIL THE SUN SINKS...

Until the sun sinks into a green
Smoke and twilight starts to spread
We speak of nothing but summer.

Yet autumn will soon tell us
The truth, in a cold voice.

A. D. HOPE, *1955*

Illness is nothing if not complicated.

THE BED

The doctor loves the patient,
The patient loves his bed;
A fine place to be born in,
The best place to be dead.

The doctor loves the patient
Because he means to die;
The patient loves the patient bed
That shares his agony.

The bed adores the doctor,
His cool and skillful touch
Soon brings another patient
Who loves her just as much.

ISAAC DE BENSERADE, *seventeenth century*

Translated by Samuel Johnson.

IN BED WE LAUGH, IN BED WE CRY

In bed we laugh, in bed we cry;
And, born in bed, in bed we die.
The near approach a bed may show
Of human bliss to human woe.

JOHN PRESS, *mid-twentieth century*

Eternal love and eternal chill: a poem can do no more than this one. Almost incongruously, words attributed to Sir Walter Raleigh come to mind: "Death and imagination; it's all the same."

WHAT THE WIND SAID

White bone clinging to white bone
In their marriage bed,
Haven and shield against menacing weather,
Shivered to hear what the wind said:
"Soon, soon, you must lie alone,
Torn like leaves from an autumn bough,
But till nightfall you may twine together
As you do now."

White bone resting on white bone
In their common grave,
Safe and sealed against menacing weather,
Were deaf to the comfort the wind gave:
"Nevermore shall you lie alone,
But close as leaves on a summer bough
Till the world's end you may twine together
As you do now."

EMPEROR CH'IEN WEN-TI, *sixth century*

We come full circle. The sentiment that began this volume will end it, a sense of longing.

WINTER NIGHT

My bed is so empty that I keep on
        waking up:
As the cold increases, the night-wind
        begins to blow.
It rustles the curtains, making a noise
        like the sea:
Oh that those were waves which could
        carry me back to you!

ACKNOWLEDGMENTS

Chao Meng-fu: "An Admonition to Myself" translated by Jonathan Chaves, from *The Columbia Book of Later Chinese Poetry*, copyright 1986 by Columbia University Press, New York. Reprinted by permission of the publisher.

J.K. Clark: "Retreat" from *The New York Times Book of Verse*, copyright 1956, 1967 by The New York Times Co. Reprinted by permission.

Gladys Ely: "Variations on Simonides" from *The New York Times Book of Verse*, copyright 1956, 1967 by The New York Times Co. Reprinted by permission.

Robert Friend: "The Hunchback" is reprinted by permission of the poet.

Suzy Q. Groden translated "The Moon Has Set" in *Poems of Sappho*, copyright 1967 by Macmillan Publishing Co. Reprinted by permission of Macmillan Publishing Co.

Anzai Hitoshi: "Sunflower" translated by Atsumi Ikuko, from *The Poetry of Postwar Japan*, 1975, edited by Kijima Hajime. Reprinted by permission of the poet.

A.D. Hope: "The Bed" from *Collected Poems 1930-1963*, copyright 1963, 1966 by A.D. Hope. Reprinted by permission of Angus and Robertson Publishers.

Wilhelm Klemm: "The Battle of the Marne" from *Contemporary German Poetry*, 1923, chosen and translated by Babette Deutch and Avrahm Yarmolinsky. Reprinted by permission of the Estate of Avrahm Yarmolinsky.

Richmond Lattimore translated "[Epicurean Conclusion]" and "For Twice Ten Years" in *Themes in Greek and Roman Epitaphs*, 1962. Reprinted by permission of the University of Illinois Press.

Archibald MacLeish: "Seafarer" from *Collected Poems 1917-1982*, copyright by the Estate of Archibald MacLeish. Reprinted by permission of Houghton Mifflin Co. All rights reserved.

Martial: "The Bee in Amber" translated by Palmer Bovie, from *Epigrams of Martial*, 1970. Reprinted by permission of Palmer Bovie.

John Masefield: "An Epilogue" from *Poems*, copyright renewed 1964 by John Masefield. Reprinted by permission of the Society of Authors as literary representative of the Estate of John Masefield.

Vladimir Mayakovsky: "Moonlit Night" from *Two Centuries of Russian Verse*, 1966, translated by Babette Deutch and edited by Avrahm Yarmolinsky. Reprinted by permission of the Estate of the editor.

Edwin Muir: "The Way" from *Collected Poems*, copyright 1960 by Willa Muir. Reprinted by permission of Oxford University Press.

Robert Nye: "A Proper Place" and "Familiar Terms" from *Darker Ends*, 1969, copyright by Robert Nye. Reprinted by permission of the poet.

Piuvkaq: "Delight in Singing" from *Eskimo Poems from Canada and Greenland*, 1973, translated by Tom Lowenstein. Reprinted by permission of Tom Lowenstein.

Ezra Pound: "In a Station of the Metro" from *Personae*, copyright 1926 by Ezra Pound. Reprinted by permission of New Directions Publishing Corp.

John Press: "Farewell" and "What the Wind Said" are reprinted by permission of the poet.

INDEX OF AUTHORS

INDEX OF FIRST LINES

ABOUT THE EDITOR

In the event Joseph Addison was right in thinking that most readers do not peruse with pleasure until they know of the editor, this brief note: The editor is a federal administrative law judge. His privilege within is an anonymous poem, entered without self-consciousness in the belief that the reader cares not whether the editor preens or rides to Hell, so long as the show is worthwhile.